Lover gurl

SHYRA VISHNOI

INDIA • SINGAPORE • MALAYSIA

ISBN
Paperback 979-8-89544-865-6
Hardcase 979-8-89556-353-3

For all the girls,

who have been in love,

Destroyed

Survived

And manages to love again.

Contents

Athazagoraphobia

(fear being forgotten by special one)

It all started when you said
We aren't that closed
And I challenged you to be

It went all night
From eleven to six in the morning
We didn't stop
Until we both saw the dawn

It all felt like meant to be
Because I felt comfortable after a long time

Still in my mind
Somewhere I am scared
Due to my previous experience
So I prepared

your virtual Head pats
Made me fall for you first
And little things you say
Just wants me to hold you close enough

You mentioned I was kissable
Just by the voice on a video
That's when I got the hope that I am still fixable

Yes, I named you MY HOE
BECAUSE maybe after that
I won't let you be anyone's
But my mine alone

This is just the beginning
But still I am frightened
that I might be just a side piece
And one day you wake up and leave me like others

I missed you today
What a lie!!
I miss you every day
With every breath I take
It's one name I say " "

the first person I am not flexing cause still feared
in my zone
That you will make me your second sad choice

It's still irritating as much
When I first met you
I woke up from dreamy eyes
And another delusional sketch drew

I hate it...every god damn minute with you
On my side
But the most of all I had ever hated
was when you weren't with me when I cried

It was sad enough that I met you in my healing
phase
Got me back where I started all this

I wanted to end it
But how can I,
When the guy in my dreams were you who kissed

Eclipse

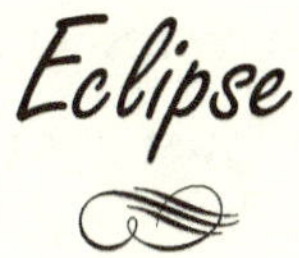

I told him
Our bond is like the moon and the sun
We depend on each other
Yet can't be together

He pointed towards the skies
And I saw my surroundings getting dark
It was the dream before I say my byes
And you left a memory mark

I see up
And noticed a solar eclipse
I was shocked in my very core
But you came while tugging my hair back with
your fingertips

You said, it's how we are
Like in hiding of the pain we endured
We represent it
Therefore I just got reassured

I mean- that was just something I only imagined
in my dreams
But you knew how to silence my screams

Redamancy

(The act of loving in return)

In the garden of our souls
Redamancy blossomed
and dancing of our heart entwined.

Euphelicia

(Happiness after wishes being granted)

I stand under night lights
And
till those stars turn into a constellation

As My silence speak for my words
You bewitched me to be yours

Air that surrounds me
was heard by all
Little did everyone know
my heart beat stopped when I saw you leaning against the wall

Before parting, you kissed me
It was hunger but forehead one was reassurance
Just like me floating over the surface of water.

Kairoclerosis

(the moment of realizing you are happy)

I came home
After you, to my actually one
With grin on my lips
And traces of your kisses hon'

The inner child of me smiling more widely
This time my broken heart was replaced with a new
This life wasn't enough to keep my love buried
But your tongue kept my mouth closed too

I was yours; you were mine
Before it all came down to separation
Until the distance between us concealed
And so was my temptation

Oblivion of sweetest were reflected in my eyes
Those lips are still felt around mine
You wiped my tear out of cries
Because you were always divine

You

Love should lift, not shatter
See the fragments of your soul scattered
Promise yourself you won't forget this
In the new upcoming moments of bliss

I saw the world in those big black eyes
But you were the one who distanced himself
Leaving me behind
All I had, was to look in the eye to see the view of myself

First love never died in me
But u came
And buried it. ALIVE

I fell in love this time
Desperately, obsessively and most of all immensely
For that cute look of your smile
I can keep my words secretly

A flower wouldn't comfort my soul
When my grave was rained upon the entire night
You destroyed me in the most beautiful way of love
But left me....to let me know
WHY STORMS ARE NAMED AFTER GOOD PEOPLE.

I have been in love before
Destroyed the next day
It was a dream all like core
But i need you the most before anyone touches my heart to play

His Eyes

His eyes was so deep and intense
I want to look at them forever or
chase them again never

I can't decide

I was damnly
so self centred
but sure when he barged in my life unannounced
he made a girl, which was his, without a doubt

I became the type of girl
That'll be hurt by him
And still look at him.
Only him

Sonnet

I beheld thee to not see my tears
Here I am, pouring my hand for you to trust
Looking at thou I didn't imagine anything for, is this could be real?
With thy soul bewitching mine to frost

A time ago, I remember to watch thy Vivacity
Which happened to take my emotions in the favour of love
Never have I desired to feel myself in it's capability
But you conquered all above

I see the birds in the sky waiting for a retort
And I will be able to hold back for Eternity
For thee to stand next to me in the honour of court
If thou decided to take my heart eternally

With the coldness of my heart, thou standing in front of me
Melting the boldness of yourself, when thou gave yourself to me

Melophile

(the one who is in love with the moon)

I was in the melody of Moon
Right above us
You were setting some music on tune
And that's all you remember about was

Thereby I am here to remind to you
That the night didn't finish with it
Because the glory of dawn was still due
When you stood up to show your outfit

till today I am here in the field of dahlia's
With the weather of rain
Sure, I want you here to be an alpha
When I want to get drenched in this season with
you again

These moments are never going to be out of my memory
Since for the first time I was the main character
If you held my hand in yours, I will live for you till century
And honour your love and respect as my treasure

Oneirataxia

(inability to distinguish between reality and fantasy)

You were standing alone
I walked to you
And looked into soul
With a future view

I poked you on your shoulder with my pen
And asked 'you angry??'
You then replied
'No' but I heard in my dreams to marry

To a doubt I asked the same question
You pat my head
and then slid an arm to my shoulder
And I was dead

It was the coldest palm
the fingers flowed a current into my body
Shivering in my soul didn't stop
Until I checked into Reality

Texts I Got to Send

Why don't you write so smthg for me?

You want me to write about you?

Don't you think so you should?

Okiee

Let me start that how great I am to have you in my fucking messed up life

It's so nice to have a person who judges you mentally not physically and the fact that you always teach me what's wrong and right, is the time i realized that I want this bond forever

We may fight a lot but at the end of the day I cry in your dms

Damn maybe you are just too important and the fact you take blames so your friend's name does not go down always gets me

And the fact that you always go with the theory "Hum saath saath hai" though sometimes irritating yet it's the right thing

I love you 3000 was our fucking thing and gonna be

until death do us apart
This paragraph is not enough since you are more awesome and great and I can write this with the surety if someone will know you by heart not by your words they'll find a reason to stay and stick with you
I always owe you

I love you 3000

I love you 3000

Tears

Wished every second of my existence
To be one of your tears

So, I could be born in your eyes
And move around your cheeks
While dying at your lips

The taste of it
Was still unknown
yet I consumed your existence

Disguised

The rain in my mind
Destroyed the grains of my heart
And still I had those guts
To ask you to kiss me in that starry night

You were the poem
And I was the poet
I wish someday you see me as the poem
As i saw you in one of mine

You were the famous art
I was the painter hiding behind
Photographs were clicked of you
While I planned on being an angel in disguised

It was the love I had before
That got me the hope to go for it again

Love Again. Ahahaha Shit

What was love for you??

LOVE?

Love.

Love.

Love. Oh my darling.

Love is the heart attack you wish for. Knowing it will cause you harm, you patiently want to experience it.

Love is a paradox you didn't wanted to believe in.

Love is the most beautiful thing to live in if it's returned otherwise the most broken thing you could have asked for.

Love is a broken glass.

It's shattered but that doesn't mean, it won't scratch you.

I hadn't mention them about you
But they saw you bathing in my eyes
They saw you in my silence
They saw you in my unspoken words
That's when I realized
The essence of it
Will never able to hide it's odour

Marmoris

(shining surface of ocean like eyes after pain)

Why is the life just a moment or two,
for this love, centuries aren't enough

So let me ask God
for some more time, a new,
I have to live just here,
I have not to go away from you

Now that you are there to share my pain,
Every pain is beautiful.

Whatever atrocity the world does to me,
in this pain, is my safety
My life became very beautiful as you stepped with me
now where else that heaven would be

My mom said
What will the world, society, people say about this?

I looked at him downstairs packing my things up
for a move in and countered
My world is him
My society is him
My people is him
I don't care what others say
I care what he says

Sirrah, Young Boy

There was I in love
But thy too busy in pretending
Tried to loathe
And here I kept my words pending

I remember to saw thy
As the sirrah near the river
Ready to Feign
In coldness from wind to make thy shiver

I reached home
To face myself in mirror
Because thy made my heart flutter
When imagine of us together

Mine surrendered on knees
Even as a lady
But thy scared to commit
And that made you shady

Seperation Phase!!!

HE WAS PULLING AWAYS IN SOME PLACE AND SOMEWHERE I WAS.

I STILL CHOSE TO CLING ONTO HIM BECAUSE THIS FEELING WAS NEVER WAS NEVER FELT ANYWHERE BUT HERE.

Mamihlapinatapai

(look shared by two, each manifesting for other)

I stared at you from across the street
As a bus came by
In seconds you were gone

I avoided you all this time
all the words fell apart
my mouth swung open
therefore I imagined of us having a new start

I was shaking,
my friend asked me about it
deep down all the recollections of emotions
flooded
where your hug stopped the earthquakes and
settled it

Another hand slid over me
felt like my own person
I turned around to notice you
and peace came to my world before I knew

Was it game
or
your eyes were true this time
because if I do fall again, it will be a crime

Full of meaning, your eyes were glowing
asking for future together
the heart chose itself over inner loath
which was promising for both

Magoa

(feeling that leaves long lasting traces)

You found beauty in decay
I found you in my silence

You captured me in your eyes
while I took you in my breath

You painted me in the canvas of your heart
and here I remembered your presence

You found to be non-existence
when in every way I saw you at distance

Agathokakological

(composed of both good and evil)

Love is the most twisted curse
I ran towards it and still you were far away

Everyone taught me to hate you
To hate villain
To hate the evil
But how can I?
When evil spelt backwards was live

HOW?
When evil had the eyes which sparkles the meaning of my life
When he had the face
Of the one, I loved the most.

Toska

(immense ache for nothing and everything all at once)

When I looked at you, there was no life
Only death
because it is where eternity lies

The most dangerous, dangerous thing was that
eye contact
but God, it was heavenly.

From each other, our eyes depart
And
an arrow felt in my silent heart

What do I do?
should I believe in that scar
or the above signs from the stars

Changing Shadows

You stood in front of me
To protect me from the Sun
As I stand in your shadows
I vowed to be your only one

I remembered you taking off your belt
Just as I spoke
'I like dominance'
Never thought that you will mistook it for violence
You gave me gift

I received it with love on my face
But the present scars became another example
About one more residing Devil in another place

Everyday I get scared,
Of what will I received today,
Will it be a strike against my face, a degrading comment or a hoe tag?
Just because I wasn't the one who betrayed

Candle

The love we had was like a candle after all
I was looking up to it's light
When it was hurting

At first I thought melting was a good sense
Until the wax burnt me
I mistook it for your cold heart
Because I wanted it to be free

I was paying for lifetime
Maybe 7 in a row
Because I committed a sin
For those seven reincarnations only on that saying
to you once hello

Princess Treatment

I laughed at your not so funny jokes
But my heart beat took a pause as I saw you in that show

The chain you gifted me
Is still tied around my wrist
Yet without you being on my side
I am always pissed

It was you
Who protected me from the sun
And every compliment like- 'she is so fine'
Was never to me none

That's smell of yours
Is still present around me in that crescent moon
And I really hope in another lifetime
I get to be yours soon

Shooting Star

I told you that I loved you
using the left over blood from my bruise
I was the just one of the many, oh you knew!
But I was the only poet with you, as their muse

I looked at you as I look at the shooting star
wishing upon as I feel my heart bloom
but you were always so far
Little did I know
the thing that I loved the most was my stars doom

Now, I love you as I love the moon
from a distance as I fall asleep under it's glitter
because it will turn into the daylight very soon
and hopefully it's unsaid 'I love you' won't make
me jitter

Boarding Life

My past life missed
The train you boarded
But I'm sure you wore
Red that day
The onset of October must've rained on
London so brutal
That your red shape shifted to orange
Each raindrop gouged holes In your scalp planting ideas
So visceral
For a new painting
Of me, In red
peeping out the window Of the train you boarded
Yeah, You and I are the same !

Heart are wildest creatures
That's why our ribs are cages
As time faded
I turned upside down, the pages

I held onto to those dreams
Until rope sliced my very skin
Sensitivity inside me suffered
As my demon gripped over the sin

I see the scars on my soul
Portrayed in the reflection of your eyes
I killed it right along
And waved a goodbye at the skies

My efforts never tried
To be in touch with my present
But I reincarnated it again
As I took my future's consent

Everything New

I should be worthy of new ears
To which your voice never reached

I should be worthy of new eyes
To which your presence wasn't captured

I should be worthy of new skin
In which you weren't engraved

I should be worthy of new lips
In which your mouth never got to kiss

Two Graves

Texting my first love
Listening to his voice again
Reading his texts again
Brings back the memories that weren't in Vain

Take me back to those times
Where you first told me your name
I would relive those moments again
Because i knew it wasn't just a game

~~For you.~~ With you. In either way
I'll dug two graves
Therefore I can slip my eternity next to you
So I can be your slave

After life is going to be a party in hell
All that I knew, my happiness was in heaven
ringing bells.

Missing Phase

I was missing him because of the delusion I made
of him and more of it,
he was coming and going out of ma' life like it
won't affect me.

Aviothic

(feeling of being in the sky)

They say- eyes don't lie
but yours told me that you loved me as you loved the dark sky,
then why did you never look at me,
and acted as if my pain you couldn't see?

I told you that I'd write you books,
but these hands shiver after every word
Was it that way my voice sounded or my looks?
Maybe it was the way I hopelessly loved you, I heard.

I was looking for the reasons to stay,
and you became one very soon,
now you haunt me every time I lay,
no one ever told me that my birth could be a doom.

Now you are poetic muse
and I'm just someone, you once met
or someone with a you-named bruise
and you are someone I loved, and love yet

Cancer

Love is
like a cancer

It enters in your heart
Uninvited

and manages
to kill you

Limerence

(state of being obsessively infatuated with someone)

I am with my friends
I think about you

Is it normal or you do too?

I am with my family,
I think about you

I HATE IT WHEN I DON'T LET MYSELF DROWN IN YOU

I listen to my playlist
I imagine you dance

I listen you as my favorite singer
And there you are with guitar

I saw my photographs
And remembered you holding that camera

I hate it that you were everywhere
even at those turns which were meant to forget
you
But more of it
I hate myself more
Who changed her path for it

Addicted

(to you)

The streets to my house are missing your visits.
I want to build a new world of our own.

Everything which is mine,
is equally yours, believe me

Inscribe your name on my breathes
It makes me feel more alive every time your heart beats.

Since, I got addicted to you!
Without you, even a moment seems like forever!

Avenoir

(urge to see your memories in advance)

I grieved about the very person who was alive
His absence has gone through me
Like a thread through a needle
Everything I have ever did
Was stitched with mixed blood of us

Basorexia

(sudden urge to kiss someone)

I was suffering from Basorexia
Every time you took your steps in front of me

Every touch of yours lingered on my skin
And suddenly I felt an obnoxious pain

A big smile and six feet height
And you left me like in the speed of light

I immortalized you from the very start
I never thought it will make us getting depart

Some feelings are better understood without words
While some experiences are better learnt from others.

False Promise!

The bird of my soul was flapping its wings
But it was not able to find the island of peace

Give me a glimpse of yours just once
Give me satisfaction, even if it's a false one

Absqualate

(to leave without saying goodbye)

We both begged!
U begged me to leave
AND
I begged for you to stay

YOU TRANSFERRED MY CHANCE TO HER
While I left stranded when you walked away

Living

I cover my ears while I sleep
I dream of us too loud
people look for their sunshine while I'm busy
gazing the thundercloud
Every time I look at you with my heart beating in
eyes
It pulls a string in me and I stay somewhere in
melancholy

You are four fingers away blooming roses in my
heart
tearing it,
soaking my lungs in blood
I sink deeper into this paradox
oblivious to what I am falling into
Maybe I'm living you instead of just loving you

Dreams Come True

You had to make all your dreams come true
As you manifested the things
You Wanted the most

Only to realise that
This time,
you visioned to be with the wrong girl

At First Sight

I was in the same place as you
But my eyes fall on you
When you looked at someone else

I fell in love at first sight
I wish
I would've laid my eyes on you twice

I was shattered by the truth
But
aura was so divine
That it made me lose my innocent youth

A part of me was
Killed to keep you breathing

A part of me was
Left behind to keep you at front

A part of me was
Hated so that you could be loved by all

A part of me was
Damaged to keep you unscratched

A part of me was
Darkened to give you light

A part of me was
Drowning, to give you wings

Trying

People asked me,
How did you punished him?
I replied
By looking everywhere except his soul

It was myth
That black eyes were shinning as moon
So to hide their charm
They were coloured by the
River of heaven' honey like you

Black- the colour of moonlight darkness
Portrayed in your eyes
Showed out of my inner self
Because I need an answer for myself previous to
clock strikes twelve

I will not let you have me without seeing the darkness that hides within me
And
I will not have you till I see the madness that makes you
If our demons cannot dance
Neither shan't we

I closed the window
No matter how beautiful the view was
I wasn't scared to walk away this time
But I turned around
To see that you didn't follow where my steps were found

You told me, I was heavenly
'the demon inside me blushes at instant'
I replied that appearances don't matter
And you touched the heart which was ready to be distant

We weren't opposite
But sure you were a drama
I loved reading fucking Shakespeare
Only this time
I didn't understand you.

Hair

People said "Hair keeps memories"
So I grew them out
Before you brushed your hand into them
Replaced the bad to good ones

You touched my hair
And sensations burned my heart into ashes
I took the scent from the air
Because another rocket in my soul crashes

Pieces of me lying on the floor
When you paced opposite of me
I never thought that the time I had
Was so unworthy

Tacenda

(things better left unsaid)

He was the only best friend I ever had,
but I was the one of those people whom would
cling to his hands to get out of the crowd.
It was never in my expectations that he would one
day be something more for me,
but sure I was one for him.

He left.....
Came back.....
Hurt me before he strides opposite to me again

I just wanted to ask him once more.
Wasn't it enough to broke me one time??
But I couldn't this time. I
couldn't heal because the mark left was last link to
what I had of him.

Cigarettes

They were more compatible with me
Than him
It was sure that the comfort I was finding in him
Was found in them
Yet I felt a piece of my heart breaking

Maybe it was the cigarettes
Or
Maybe it was him who left me broken

Anagesis

(falling out of love)

I believed in our love
Until he touched
And all my butterflies were dead
All this time I thought I LOVED HIM
But it was his delusion I made of him in which I was in love with

Kashvika leaned at my side and said~
Sometimes your heart needs more time to accept what your mind already knows.

Page by Page

I still remember
My favourite book was burning page by page
And all the pieces of my heart which were bandaged by it
Started to break as well

Strangers

I knew
His favourite food
His favourite colour
His favourite song
His nicknames
His fears
His favourite girl
And even his darkest secrets yet
YET
he was a strangers to me

Space B/W Us

Hope was with me
all along
But you cut ties thus
Created a SPACE BETWEEN US

Hope!

I fell in love with hope over here when I knew he wasn't going to follow me.

Still somewhere I wanted him too no matter how much I deny it.

He was reflecting in every image and it wounded me every time to bring me back to reality.

Hope

He came into my life
like a thunder on waves

I slipped myself
to flow away
in hope

Only to dig myself
A Grave

Librocubicularis

(person who reads in bed)

I love poetry because there is no correct way to
read it or even write it. I could say
"Those eyes were a war that I don't mind dying in."
And still people will get the feeling behind it.
Emotions behind it.

Chapters

I thought my book was over
And you came along
Revived it.
Thus giving me the chapters
For which, I long-awaited

I was full of debts of broken hearts
In those eyes, you made me the queen of universe
And I told you
That's not my feelings works

Butterflies in my stomach whispered
-you lied.

Destined to Be Together by Death

Even in death, I'd recognize your soul
FIND ME IN THE STARS.

WE'LL BE THE NEXT GENERATIONS OF
CONSTELLATIONS.

I looked at the reflection
Only to be see that you were peaking
I turned around
And found out that I was dreaming

I was killing myself
To give us a life.
I was saving the very person
Who was pushing my head underwater

That sombre feeling
Ran in my view
Mixed with my own blood
As I heard those stories you went through

Fragile, we were
Things that were meant to keep us alive
Can be the one to destroy us too
Therefore I tried my best to survive

Seijaku

(solitude isn't loneliness)

No matter what happened
I chose myself in that position
To get my self-respect down
Only in one hope that he will love once me

It was like sitting in a burning house
Because it was home to me
It was close to missing the dead person
Who was one close to me.

Litrost

(a state of agony)

When love has lost it's meaning
And
No one to hear your heart screaming

When your eyes cry pain
And
everything you say goes in vain

With no purpose in life
And
Day that mould into the night

While all you can do is wait
And
Those retched memories gushing through Gate

Why was I there
When he was destined to be elsewhere

Oh, you fucking heart
You betrayed me
Making it difficult
For me to be free

Exulansis

(Giving up talking about an experience to which people can't relate)

He healed the parts that were never broken by him
and broke some which I never thought he will.

He was my infinite sky,
and I was that bird flapping my wings to edge.

For him I was always that beautiful view inside an empty box.
He saw me as an empty person,
but filled with his love and care
like moon does to sun

Aging i

My eyes are stuck looking at him
My teeth are unable to cut a silky thread

My age has become white since a long time
But this black cover of youth
doesn't go away

By God, my heartbeat
has gone faster

The colour of my face
is slowly disappearing
I'm scared of sleeping alone

Oh my heart, is still in its childhood even I was old
and on my own

Isophilia

(desired to be alone)

Open the window to your heart
I'll open the door for mine.

Des VU

(awareness of a current moment to become memory)

Which one is my real home?

There were two roads
leading me

one was
to home

other was to
my shallow grave

{I was actually in the middle of the road; trying to figure out, should I take left or right because one leads to home and other, to another hope}

Reason Behind My Smile

My love,
you must have met millions like me
But I only found you

you're the reason behind the big smile on my lips
Look what has happened to me
By bringing you in my dream

Deserved Better!

On my lips, it was dark cherry tint.
Sometimes a note it was
Sometimes a hint.

I, not only let go of my past,
but also sacrificed the future of us together

So once more in my life, I will not be found crying
over someone
who very well destroyed me at the end

Wise Words 1

A tear slipped when I said~
I was looking into his eyes and then
HE WAS GONE.
I died in that very moment

The lady on my side whispered ~
Very few people get lucky, to die,
While looking into their loved ones eyes

Now I feel stupid
because I didn't notice the Cupid
Among us was the space
that was never filled even though I felt safe

People say "death is forever "
Thus I want to be dead with you on my side
So, I can be the one in surrender
for me to show off in hell with pride

This wasn't just my feelings
But millions of us are out there enduring the same thing
I kept on Shaking hands with Hades for all the dealings
Because he knew how much I wanted to be yours in vain

Every feeling I felt talking to him
Is. Was. Relating to his heart.
Believe me or not, he wanted my suffering to get trim
Because he once felt the same tart

Killed Me!

Leaving you almost killed me

But

Staying with you literally killed me

Words to Myself

Please don't try to change my mind
If you try to make me understand

I will give in
And
If I do that
I will fall apart with my face buried in my hand

We can't choose whom to fall in love with
But
We can choose to walk away from it to end the
myth

Yaunfen

(relationship brought by destiny)

If appearances are more beautiful than soul
that why I await for you in heaven
when I know your physical self will be burnt into ashes

Reality:)

This was the truth that I was avoiding all along.
I was just another girl he lied too, just this time it went on for two years.

Mustpouffer

(mysterious sound heard over the ocean)

I'm a refugee
like a butterfly from violence
I stop for just a moment
While in the next moment I fly
I'm like a narrow lane
In searching for the path to heaven
Wherever You'll turn,
I'll turn in the same direction
I want to be a part of Your caravan
As to become a better person before I finish my life span

Things I Wanted

I wish I was a narcissist
I could have been
My own poem
My own art
Why need someone else
To do things that you can do by yourself

Don't ever judge on what's inside in the book
Sometimes lines and metaphors have different meanings

Worth It?

I was chasing after someone who was running
away from me
&
looking back to make sure that I was still there.

Metonia

(journey of changing one self, mind, heart,
way of life, etc)

My heart was in three thousand pieces
Each of them had one perspective

Even if someone else was at fault
I'll rather clean the knife from which they stabbed
And return it
For me it was 'they had their reasons'

I was so much worse
But time changed me like anything
My words were sealed behind my smile
And my soul was finding the perfect ring

Wants?

Out of all the people I had in my life
My heart paused for the one who never looked at
me the way I wanted him

Scriptuent

(consuming the passion to write)

Was there any value to this thing we call it
"living"?
I guess not I loved you so much
but at the end
Why was I the other woman when I was with you
And she who was miles away was in your heart

Seen just now

Left me on read huh?

La Dour Exquise

(exquisite pain)

Walked together like parallel lines
never intersected but still promised
to be there for each other till eternity

Was only I believing to the real truth or your way to
show me your real face??

Scared of my love for you
because I know it will destroy me like before

And stupid soul inside me that I thought died
and very much let it.

In Hiding!

Thy are mine
I hereby confirm
how much thy escape, I see
hence this event would not take place

Pretty liars hide their faces
Pretty souls hide their intentions

I don't know what was I hiding,
Was it my feelings or your truth?.

Phosphemes

(stars you see after rubbing your eyes)

Chattering is halfwit's pursuit

Your eyes can't hide
what are words conceal

A tear slipped away....
He countered

My gawd!
Your tears a loyal
Without consent they don't even shed

I stopped myself from falling them down again

Don't imprison them
let them be free as well

He considered us as friends
I hated that

Kashvika said....
Love has obsession
But
Friendship has peacefulness

Chaos in my words
As I pulled myself closer

Love, which was meant to give me a life
~~Leaving.~~ Ended up my heart slaughtered

Kalopsia

(delusion being better than reality)

Never cried because of you
You are not worth it

I cried because of the delusion I made of you
Nonetheless
soon you shattered it with truth

None Left

I wanted him to love me
But I don't want to hold on to me anymore
I loved him enough in the past
That I can't let myself go through any longer

I was never a whore
Neither I wish to be aesthetic
But my unheard dying wishes
Are making me pathetic

I literally get the meaning of the quote
'The giver gives so much that he himself gets empty inside'
And all I'm doing was
Telling myself that it had been applied

This goes on and on, because my brain says to
hold on to him
But my heart Refuses to do so
In my world where I kept him so above
I forgot to give myself the credit I deserve

Too Much

Sometimes, we ruin things
By loving too much

Sometimes, we ruin things
By CARING too much

Ink Dried like the Blood in My Veins!

Every time, somewhere, a pen drips
from the hand of someone who once loved,
and here I am for about half an hour,
whose paper was blank and pen was dried

The fact that you have no clue
how much this pen had written
the poems published on it's Ink

My brain was fucked up
to my feelings for you
that either too much or too less,
I can't decide if it was a mess

Love is a four letter word.
Hate is a four letter word.
It's for you to decide what you own
A broken heart
Or
An upcoming revenge

Back Story or Front Story!!

Reading the book backward or forward
Either way we turned out to be strangers

Fictophile

(in love with fictional men)

Pain is when
Your heart fells for a person
Who was only available through paper and ink
And limited till 315 pages of your life

Scars

You got scars honey?

That's just something my cat did. You don't worry

Little did she knew that I used the same blade to
cut myself
and the scars she had were same as mine

Words You Wanted to Hear

Girl, if you are reading this
We get it
We all know your love wasn't stupid
Wasn't cringe
Your one sided was enough true to get yourself left alone
That's why we are here for you
Always and forever
Just so you know, there is someone out there who will die for 1/10 of your love

If the slightest chance anyone making you feel like that your love wasn't love
Don't listen to it
Love is a calm sea with heavy tides
You just have to embrace yourself enough to get through this one more time

Remember about you being yourself as a child and
everyone you loved once loved your little things
but as you grew up
They changed.
They left you.
Just once more you have to make yourself reach to
the other side and we will be waiting for you there
The most beautiful thing about your love was that
it was one sided....you don't need him otherwise
your greatest story will always be incomplete.
It's better to be in your delulu than to snap into
the reality you never wanted to believe in.

Elysian

(divinely inspired)

Whatever between you and him
Was just a character development
Not it's for you decide
Was it for you or him??

World Today

In a world where
marriage is only security

In a world where
ring on hand is just a broken condom

In a world where
A ring in a box is just the snake below

In a world where
proposal is just a handcuff

In a world where
where I immortalized you

Blood

He says his favorite color is red
So i bleed myself to death
Just to be his favorite

Just for once,
To be loved by this so perfection

THOSE WHO DREAM BY DAY ARE COGNIZANT OF MANY

THINGS WHICH ESCAPE THOSE WHO DREAM ONLY BY NIGHT.

After all girls complete each other

I left one page for you girls

add your 100th

AND COMPLETE ME

About the Book

Lovergurl is not about a gurl who falls in love but it is about a gurl who fell in love, got her heart broken and somehow had the strength to find "The One." It was honestly my best journey writing a book about the gurls I met who bandaged their loved ones but were thrown away as soon as they were used.

This book leads on with love which were epic, then the heart break which were more intense and end with true love feelings with the hint of first love reminders.

I wish I could point out poems to the people from I have wrote them for but honestly let them be anonymous. I know while reading this book, they must be blushing at those pages which were once closed in my heart.

Surely cracks flooded my body with blood
and left traces like on mud.

There are people in my life who went through once in a lifetime like I did and I can proudly call them out since they endured the same heart break.

Note from Author

An author with many ideas but limited time to work.

Heya,

I am Shyra Vishnoi, who is a poetess and an author. I really hope you guys would love another book of mine which is work in progress. In my opinion, I still think everyone has a potential of writing in themselves and that never shows itself until one is in the same place as me.

I mean, it is such an honor for me that a pretty gurl like you chose my heart break journey to read and all my hard work credit goes to my friends and family who listened to my poem and appreciated my writing career.

I have never taken a writing course but still I managed to portray my feelings in simple words. I hope one day, you, gurl pick up a pen too and start pouring out your feelings on the paper like I did.

As a writer, I was going crazy to see my lovers reciting and completing the poems that I have been stuck on.

I am sorry to break your heart readers but no matter how many times I will write that I have moved on from my first love, he will always be my first love.

If you, gurl have a story for me to write about.

Do email on- vishnoishyra@gmail.com

Acknowledgements

I sincerely want to thank my English teacher, Mrs. Manisha Badoni mam who taught me Shakespeare and somehow actually made him one of my favorite playwriter. She raised me like her own child and till this day. And I, who used to fail in English still think of her as my own mother. Her encouragement to explore the nuances of each play have not only enhanced my understanding of the subject but have also ignited a genuine interest in the beauty of Shakespeare's language and the timeless relevance of his work.

She, who was my class teacher and my second mom before that heard my cries, gave me solutions to my problems and still once in a while checks on me. If it isn't enough, I hope one day I get the courage to tell her how much I love her.

Ilesha Rawat, my soul sister she is. I met her in my broken phase and she was the one who brought me back to my feet from kneels. She got me off from my toxic friends and headed me to a new start. New beginning.

Another soulmate in my life is Saanvi Sethi. I am still a baby to her whom she can mommy up. To this day, she is my inspiration who sat with me at my lunch when everyone was running away.

My special thanks will always go to Shroy Karanwal. The person who went through the same heartbreak as mine just after few months. I wasn't just babysitting myself but he made me registered in motherhood.

Kashvika Pant, my another babygurl. I love her so damn much but yeah, irritating habits never stops. She is so adorable but stupid at the same time. To the reality the lines she said where my daily dose to get over someone.

www.ingramcontent.com/pod-product-compliance
Lightning Source LLC
LaVergne TN
LVHW091059150826
845673LV00002B/642

* 9 7 9 8 8 9 5 4 4 8 6 5 6 *